A Midsummer Night's Dream

The Shorter Shakespeare

Adapted from William Shakespeare by Tracy Irish

CAREL Inspire Learning

carelpress.co.uk

Guthrie Theater, photo: Michal Daniel

Cover: Mustardseed (Kristin Shirilla) in Orlando Shakespeare's A Midsummer Night's Dream (2011) photo: Tony Firriolo
Page one: Titania & Bottom (Sarah Ireland and Michael Daly) in Orlando Shakespeare's A Midsummer Night's Dream (2011) photo: Tony Firriolo

Published by Carel Press Ltd
4 Hewson Street
Carlisle CA2 5AU
Tel 01228 538928

office@carelpress.co.uk
www.carelpress.co.uk

© Tracy Irish and Carel Press 2003
Reprinted 2006; Reprinted in colour 2012, 2015

All rights are reserved. No part of this book may be reproduced or transmitted, in any form or by any means, without permission.

For permission to give a public performance of this play please write to Carel Press.
(No fee will be charged for a performance in a school or youth club unless an admission charge is made, however, permission is still required.)

ISBN 978 1 872365 87 9

Printed by Interpress Budapest

Characters

Two modern narrators introduce, explain and describe the action

Nobles

Theseus	Duke of Athens	**Hermia**	in love with Lysander
Hippolyta	Queen of the Amazons about to marry Theseus	**Lysander**	} both want to
		Demetrius	} marry Hermia
Egeus	Hermia's father	**Helena**	in love with Demetrius

Workmen

(and their characters in *Pyramus and Thisbe*)

Quince	carpenter (Prologue)	**Starveling**	tailor (Moonshine)
Bottom	weaver (Pyramus)	**Snout**	tinker (Wall)
Flute	bellows mender (Thisbe)	**Snug**	joiner (Lion)

Fairies

Oberon	King of the fairies	**Peaseblossom**	}
Titania	Queen of the fairies	**Cobweb**	}
		Moth	} servants of Titania
Puck	Oberon's servant	**Mustardseed**	}
		Fairy	}

Various other human & fairy attendants

Titania and Oberon, Royal Exchange Theatre, Manchester, photo: Steven Vaughan

Contents

Act 1 Scene 1 5
Act 1 Scene 2 12
Act 2 Scene 1 16
Act 2 Scene 2 23
Act 3 Scene 1 28
Act 3 Scene 2 33
Act 4 Scene 1 48
Act 4 Scene 2 54
Act 5 Scene 1 56
Act 5 Scene 2 66

Hermia, Lysander and Demetrius (Michele Vazquez, Avery Clark and Walter Kmiec) in Orlando Shakespeare's A Midsummer Night's Dream (2011) photo: Tony Firriolo

Act 1 Scene 1

The Royal Palace in Athens, Ancient Greece

Narrators come in. They remain on stage as audience throughout the performance

Narrator 1: Hey we're going on holiday to Crete this year – sun, sea, sand. I can't wait!

Narrator 2: And legends – that's where Theseus beat the Minotaur.

Narrator 1: Huh – who beat what?

Narrator 2: You know, the Minotaur – a monster, half man, half bull? Had a habit of eating children until Theseus killed it.

Narrator 1: Oh yeah, I think I've heard of that. So that was on Crete was it? This Theseus lived on Crete?

Narrator 2: No, he was just visiting. The children were sent every year from Athens because the Athenians were afraid of the Minotaur. Theseus killed the Minotaur, saved the children and soon after became the king of Athens.

Narrator 1: He was a bit of a hero then?

Narrator 2: Definitely. He fought other famous battles too – including one against an army of warrior women called Amazons. Theseus fell in love with their Queen. Her name was Hippolyta and she agreed to marry him. They appear in a Shakespeare play.

Narrator 1: Shakespeare? Hey, I was telling you about my holiday in the sun and now we're talking about Ancient Greek heroes and William Shakespeare?

Narrator 2: Yeah, it's a great story – A Midsummer Night's Dream.

Narrator 1: I've heard of that too. It's about fairies, right?

Narrator 2: There are fairies in it, that's true. Wait, let me find the play.

Narrator 2 gets a book and opens it

That's right, the story begins in Theseus' palace in Athens, a few days before his marriage to Hippolyta.

Theseus and Hippolyta come in talking and laughing together, attended by servants

Theseus: Hippolyta I wooed thee with my sword,
And won thy love doing thee injuries,
But I will wed thee in another key –
With pomp, with triumph, and with revelling.

Act 1 Scene 1

Narrator 2: But the play's not really about them. It's about four of their wealthy subjects. It's a bit complicated but there's a young man called Demetrius who wants to marry a young woman called Hermia.

Narrator 1: What's complicated about that?

Narrator 2: Well Hermia doesn't want to marry Demetrius. She doesn't love him. She loves Lysander.

Narrator 1: Oh, I see. Does this Lysander love Hermia?

Narrator 2: Oh yes.

Narrator 1: Well that's okay then. They can marry each other and ignore Demetrius.

Narrator 2: No. Remember that this is ancient Greece – or Shakespeare's version of ancient Greece anyway.

Narrator 1: So?

Narrator 2: Well Hermia's father – he's called Egeus – he wants her to marry Demetrius.

Narrator 1: Why?

Narrator 2: No good reason really. But in those days a girl had to marry whoever her father chose.

Narrator 1: So what did they do?

Narrator 2: Well, Egeus took Hermia, and Lysander and Demetrius, to Theseus to sort it out.

Egeus comes in, pulling his daughter, Hermia with him. They are followed by Lysander and Demetrius. Egeus bows to Theseus

Egeus: Full of vexation come I, with complaint
Against my child, my daughter, Hermia.
Stand forth Demetrius. My noble lord,
This man hath my consent to marry her.
Stand forth Lysander. And, my gracious Duke,
This hath bewitched the bosom of my child.

Turning to Lysander

With cunning hast thou filched my daughter's heart,
Turned her obedience which is due to me
To stubborn harshness.

Turning back to Theseus

And my gracious Duke,
Be it so she will not here before your grace
Consent to marry with Demetrius,

I beg the ancient privilege[1] of Athens:
As she is mine, I may dispose of her,
Which shall be either to this gentleman
Or to her death, according to our law.

Theseus: What say you Hermia? Be advised fair maid.
To you your father should be as a god.
Demetrius is a worthy gentleman.

Hermia: So is Lysander.

Theseus: In himself he is,
But in this kind[2], wanting your father's voice[3],
The other must be held the worthier.

Hermia: I would my father looked but with my eyes.

Theseus: Rather your eyes must with his judgement look.

Hermia: I do beseech your grace that I may know
The worst that may befall me in this case
If I refuse to wed Demetrius.

Theseus: Either to die the death or to abjure[4]
For ever the society of men.
To live a barren sister[5] all your life;
Chanting faint hymns at the cold fruitless moon.
Take time to pause, and by the next new moon –
The sealing[6] day betwixt my love and me –
Upon that day either prepare to die
For disobedience to your father's will,
Or else to wed Demetrius, as he would[7],
Or on Diana's[8] altar to protest
For aye[9] austerity and single life.

Demetrius: Relent sweet Hermia, and Lysander, yield
Thy crazed title to my certain right.

Lysander: You have her father's love, Demetrius,
Let me have Hermia's. Do you marry him.

---

[1] traditional right [2] case [3] without your father's approval [4] give up [5] nun [6] wedding
[7] wishes [8] the followers of Diana, goddess of the moon, took vows of chastity [9] ever

Act 1 Scene 1 — *The Shorter Shakespeare*

Hermia pleads with Theseus, RSC production, photo: Stewart Hemley © Royal Shakespeare Company

Egeus: Scornful Lysander! True, he hath my love,
And she is mine, and all my right of her
I do estate unto Demetrius.

Lysander: *(to Theseus)* I am, my lord, as well derived as he.
My fortunes every way as fairly ranked,
And – which is more than all these boasts can be –
I am beloved of beauteous Hermia.
Demetrius – I'll avouch it to his head –
Made love to Nedar's daughter, Helena,
And won her soul, and she, sweet lady, dotes
Devoutly dotes, dotes in idolatry
Upon this spotted[1] and inconstant man.

Theseus: I must confess that I have heard so much.
But you, fair Hermia, look you arm yourself
To fit your fancies to your father's will,
Or else the law of Athens yields you up

---

[1] dishonourable, with a stain on his character

The Shorter Shakespeare   *Act 1 Scene 1*

                 To death or to a vow of single life.
                 Come my Hippolyta, what cheer my love?
                 Demetrius and Egeus, go along.
                 I must employ you in some business.

Egeus: With duty and desire we follow you.

Theseus leads Hippolyta out, followed by Demetrius and Egeus and all the attendants. Lysander and Hermia are left alone

Narrator 1: So Lysander was saying that Demetrius had been playing around with another girl called Helena?

Narrator 2: More than playing around. He was engaged to her. Then he changed his mind and decided he preferred Hermia.

Narrator 1: And yet Helena still loves him?

Narrator 2: Oh yes. And to make matters worse, Helena and Hermia are best friends – or at least they have been up until now.

Narrator 1: Helena must feel awful! It's bad enough to be rejected, but the man she loves is planning to marry her best friend!

Narrator 2: And Hermia has to decide whether to give up Lysander and marry Demetrius or to become a nun or to die.

Narrator 1: Surely there must be a way around this.

Lysander: How now my love? Why is your cheek so pale?
             How chance the roses there do fade so fast?

Hermia: Belike for want of rain, which I could well
          Beteem[1] them from the tempest of my eyes.

Lysander: Ay me, for aught that I could ever read,
             Could ever hear by tale or history,
             The course of true love never did run smooth.

Hermia: O hell! – to choose love by another's eyes.

Lysander puts his arm around Hermia to comfort her

Lysander: Hear me, Hermia, I have a widow aunt,
             And she respects me as her only son.
             From Athens is her house remote seven leagues.
             There, gentle Hermia, may I marry thee,
             And to that place the sharp Athenian law
             Cannot pursue us. If thou lov'st me then,

---

[1] pour down on

Steal forth thy father's house tomorrow night,
And in the wood, a league without[1] the town,
There will I stay for thee.

Hermia: My good Lysander,
I swear to thee by Cupid's strongest bow,
By his best arrow with the golden head,
By the simplicity of Venus' doves,[2]
By that which knitteth souls and prospers loves,
By all the vows that ever men have broke –
In number more than ever women spoke –
In that same place thou hast appointed me
Tomorrow truly will I meet with thee.

Lysander: Keep promise, love. Look here comes Helena.

Helena comes in

Hermia: God speed, fair Helena. Whither away?

Helena: Call you me fair? That 'fair' again unsay.
Demetrius loves your fair – O happy fair!
Your eyes are lodestars[3], and your tongue's sweet air
More tuneable than lark to shepherd's ear.
O teach me how you look, and with what art
You sway the motion of Demetrius' heart.

Hermia: I frown upon him, yet he loves me still.

Helena: O that your frowns would teach my smiles such skill!

Hermia: I give him curses, yet he gives me love.

Helena: O that my prayers could such affection move!

Hermia: The more I hate the more he follows me.

Helena: The more I love, the more he hateth me.

Hermia: His folly, Helen is no fault of mine.

Helena: None but your beauty; would that fault were mine!

Hermia: Take comfort. He no more shall see my face.
Lysander and myself will fly this place.

---

[1] outside [2] Venus' chariot was pulled by doves – birds which mate for life [3] guiding stars

Lysander: Helen, to you our minds we will unfold.
Tomorrow night, when Phoebe[1] doth behold
Her silver visage[2] in the watery glass,
Decking with liquid pearl the bladed grass –
A time that lovers' flights doth still conceal –
Through Athens' gates we have devised to steal.

Hermia: And in the wood where often you and I
Upon faint primrose beds were wont to lie,
Emptying our bosoms of their counsel[3] sweet,
There my Lysander and myself shall meet,
And thence from Athens turn away our eyes
To seek new friends and stranger companies.
Farewell sweet playfellow. Pray thou for us,
And good luck grant thee thy Demetrius.

Hermia and Lysander say goodbye to Helena and run off

Helena: How happy some o'er other some can be!
Through Athens I am thought as fair as she.
But what of that? Demetrius thinks not so.
He will not know what all but he do know.
Love looks not with the eyes but with the mind,
And therefore is winged Cupid painted blind[4].
For ere Demetrius looked on Hermia's eyne[5]
He hailed down oaths that he was only mine,
And when this hail some heat from Hermia felt,
So he dissolved, and showers of oaths did melt.
I will go tell him of fair Hermia's flight.
Then to the wood will he tomorrow night
Pursue her, and for this intelligence
If I have thanks it is a dear expense.

Helena runs off to find Demetrius

---

[1] Diana, the moon [2] face [3] sharing our secrets [4] Cupid is often shown blindfolded (so his arrows of love could fly anywhere) [5] eyes

Act 1 Scene 2

Peter Quince's house

As the Narrators speak, the scene changes and on to the stage come Quince, the carpenter, Snug, the joiner, Bottom, the weaver, Flute, the bellows-mender, Snout, the tinker and Starveling, the tailor. The men quietly greet each other and settle down

Narrator 1: Oh dear, so Lysander and Hermia are going to run away together and get married – but it's a shame they told Helena about it – she's going to tell Demetrius, isn't she? Just to get a bit of his attention.

Narrator 2: That's about it! And the four lovers are all going to end up in the wood outside Athens tonight. But they won't be alone. This lot will be there – the ordinary men of Athens. They lead very different lives to Theseus and the lovers, working hard at their various trades to earn a living. They've decided to put together a play, in the hope that Theseus will want to see it as part of his wedding celebrations.

Narrator 1: Is that because they like Theseus?

Narrator 2: That, and the fact that if he likes their play, they might get a reward.

Narrator 1: So why will they end up in the wood?

Narrator 2: It's a quiet place to rehearse.

Quince: Is all our company here?

Bottom: You were best to call them generally[1], man by man, according to the scrip.

Quince: Here is the scroll of every man's name, which is thought fit, through all Athens, to play in our interlude before the Duke and the Duchess on his wedding-day at night.

Bottom: First, good Peter Quince, say what the play treats on[2]; then read the names of the actors, and so grow to a point.

Quince: Marry, our play is, 'The most lamentable comedy, and most cruel death of Pyramus and Thisbe.'

---

[1] Bottom means individually. He often uses words incorrectly   [2] is about

The Shorter Shakespeare   *Act 1 Scene 2*

Bottom: A very good piece of work, I assure you, and a merry. Now, good Peter Quince, call forth your actors by the scroll.

Quince: Answer as I call you. Nick Bottom, the weaver.

Bottom: Ready. Name what part I am for, and proceed.

Quince: You, Nick Bottom, are set down for Pyramus.

Bottom: What is Pyramus? a lover, or a tyrant?

Quince: A lover, that kills himself most gallantly for love.

Bottom: That will ask some tears in the true performing of it. If I do it, let the audience look to their eyes; I will move stones. Yet my chief humour is for a tyrant.

Bottom stands up and makes a dramatic speech

> The raging rocks
> And shivering shocks
> Shall break the locks
> Of prison gates.
> And Phibbus' car
> Shall shine from far
> And make and mar
> The foolish Fates.[1]

The other men are impressed and applaud.

Bottom: This was lofty! Now name the rest of the players. *(To the other men)* This is a tyrant's vein; a lover is more condoling[2].

Quince: Francis Flute, the bellows-mender.

Flute: Here, Peter Quince.

Quince: You must take Thisbe on you.

Flute: What is Thisbe? A wandering knight?

Quince: It is the lady that Pyramus must love.

Flute: Nay, faith, let not me play a woman – I have a beard coming.

---

[1] the whole speech is nonsense but sounds impressive   [2] Bottom is proud of his ability to act in the style of a tyrant but is also sure he can play more emotional roles

Act 1 Scene 2				The Shorter Shakespeare

Flute, Snug, Bottom, Starveling, Snout and Quince (Christopher Kiley, Matt Wenge, Michael Daly, Mason Criswell, Trent Fucci and Anne Hering) in Orlando Shakespeare's A Midsummer Night's Dream (2011) photo: Tony Firriolo

Quince: That's all one. You shall play it in a mask, and you may speak as small as you will.

Bottom: An[1] I may hide my face, let me play Thisbe too. I'll speak in a monstrous little voice, *(speaking in a high voice)* 'Ah, Pyramus, my lover dear.'

Quince: No, no, you must play Pyramus, and Flute, you Thisbe.

Bottom: Well, proceed.

Quince: Robin Starveling, the tailor.

Starveling: Here, Peter Quince.

Quince: Robin Starveling, you must play Thisbe's mother. Tom Snout, the tinker.

Snout: Here, Peter Quince.

Quince: You, Pyramus's father; myself, Thisbe's father; Snug, the joiner, you the lion's part[2]: and, I hope, here is a play fitted.

Snug: Have you the lion's part written? Pray you, if it be, give it me, for I am slow of study.

Quince: It is nothing but roaring.

Bottom: Let me play the lion too. I will roar that I will make the duke say, 'Let him roar again, let him roar again.'

Quince: An you should do it too terribly you would fright the duchess and the ladies that they would shriek, and that were enough to hang us all.

All: That would hang us, every mother's son.

Quince: You can play no part but Pyramus; for Pyramus is a sweet-faced man; a most lovely, gentleman-like man. Therefore, you must needs play Pyramus.

Bottom: Well, I will undertake it.

Quince: Masters, here are your parts and I am to entreat you,

---

[1] if [2] the lion's part usually means the biggest share

request you, and desire you, to con[1] them by tomorrow night, and meet me in the palace wood, a mile without the town, by moonlight. There will we rehearse; for if we meet in the city, we shall be dogged with company, and our devices known. I pray you, fail me not.

Bottom: We will meet and there we may rehearse most obscenely and courageously. Take pains; be perfect. Adieu.

All the men walk off, talking or studying their scripts

Act 2 Scene 1

A wood near Athens

As the Narrators speak, they move from one side of the stage to the other and the scene changes

Narrator 1: Well, they were an entertaining bunch those workmen.

Narrator 2: They're sometimes called the 'mechanicals'.

Narrator 1: Is that like a car mechanic?

Narrator 2: Mechanics or mechanicals in Shakespeare's day meant a craftsman who worked with his hands.

Narrator 1: And the weaver, Bottom, he's a bit of a show off, but all his friends seem to think he's great.

Narrator 2: And they think he's clever for using long words but he keeps using them in the wrong places. We'll catch up with them again later. Meanwhile, can you remember what you said the play was about?

Narrator 1: Fairies?

Narrator 2: This is the wood where the fairy folk live and the lovers and the mechanicals are heading for it. Here comes one of them, Robin Goodfellow or Puck as he's also known.

Narrator 1: And here comes another one.

Puck comes in from one direction and a fairy comes in from another

Puck: How now, spirit, whither wander you?

---

[1] learn, know

Fairy: Over hill, over dale,
Thorough bush, thorough briar,
Over park, over pale,
Thorough flood, thorough fire.
I do wander everywhere
Swifter than the moon's sphere,
And I serve the Fairy Queen
To dew her orbs upon the green.[1]

Puck: The king doth keep his revels here tonight.
Take heed the queen come not within his sight.

Puck and the fairy move back but continue to talk

Narrator 1: Looks like the fairy king doesn't like the fairy queen?

Narrator 2: They have been quarrelling because the queen, Titania, has brought back a little boy from India. He was the son of her friend, an Indian queen, who died in childbirth. People believe fairies often steal human children and leave goblins in their place. So this child is one of those, a changeling.

Narrator 1: And the king doesn't like the boy?

Narrator 2: Oh no, the king, he's called Oberon, is jealous. He wants the boy to be his own pageboy and he also wants all Titania's love for himself. The arguments between them are causing problems and upsetting things in the human world.

Narrator 1: In our world? Why?

Narrator 2: Because the fairies, especially the king and queen, look after the natural world. They make everything work in harmony. When they are quarrelling there is bad weather, the seasons are disrupted and that means disaster for the countryside.

Puck and the fairy move forward again

Puck: And now they never meet in grove or green,
By fountain clear, or spangled starlight sheen,
But they do square[2], that all their elves for fear
Creep into acorn cups, and hide them there.

The fairy now realises that she recognises Puck

Fairy: Either I mistake your shape and making[3] quite
Or else you are that shrewd and knavish sprite

---

[1] sprinkle fairy rings in the grass with dew   [2] quarrel, fight   [3] appearance

>   Called Robin Goodfellow. Are not you he
>   That frights the maidens of the villagery?
>   Are not you he?

Puck: Thou speak'st aright.
           I am that merry wanderer of the night.

Oberon comes in from one direction and Titania comes in from another. They are both followed by various attendants

>   But make room, fairy, here comes Oberon.

Fairy: And here my mistress. Would that he were gone.

Oberon: Ill met by moonlight, proud Titania.

Titania: What, jealous Oberon? Fairies, skip hence.
            I have forsworn his bed and company.

Photo: Carol Rosegg. Shakespeare Theatre, Washington, USA 1999. Andrew Long as Oberon, Valerie Leonard as Titania and (in background) Blair Singer as Puck. Director: Joe Calarco.

The Shorter Shakespeare   *Act 2 Scene 1*

Oberon: Tarry, rash wanton[1]. Am not I thy lord?

Titania: Then, I must be thy lady; but I know
When thou hast stolen away from fairy land,
And in the shape of Corin sat all day,
Playing on pipes of corn, and versing love
To amorous Phillida[2]. Why art thou here,
Come from the furthest steppe of India?
But that the Amazon, your warrior love,
To Theseus must be wedded, and you come
To give their bed joy and prosperity.

Oberon: How canst thou thus for shame, Titania,
Glance at my credit[3] with Hippolyta,
Knowing I know thy love to Theseus?

Titania: These are the forgeries[4] of jealousy,
And never, since the middle summer's spring[5],
Met we on hill, in dale, forest, or mead,
By paved fountain, or by rushy brook,
Or in the beached margin of the sea,
To dance our ringlets to the whistling wind,
But with thy brawls thou hast disturbed our sport.

Oberon: Do you amend it then. It lies in you.
Why should Titania cross her Oberon?
I do but beg a little changeling boy
To be my henchman.[6]

Titania: Set your heart at rest.
The fairy land buys not the child of me.
His mother was a votaress of my order,[7]
And in the spiced Indian air by night,
Full often hath she gossiped by my side,
And sat with me on Neptune's yellow sands,
But she, being mortal, of that boy did die.
And for her sake I do rear up her boy,
And for her sake I will not part with him.

---

[1] wait, you rebellious, unfaithful woman   [2] Titania complains that Oberon takes on a human form to flirt with humans, including Hippolyta   [3] comment on how much Hippolyta thinks of me   [4] lies   [5] beginning   [6] pageboy   [7] priestess of my religion

Oberon: How long within this wood intend you stay?

Titania: Perchance, till after Theseus' wedding day.
If you will patiently dance in our round,
And see our moonlight revels, go with us.
If not, shun me, and I will spare your haunts.[1]

Oberon: Give me that boy, and I will go with thee.

Titania: Not for thy fairy kingdom. Fairies, away!

Titania and all her attendants leave

Oberon: Well, go thy way. Thou shalt not from this grove
Till I torment thee for this injury.
My gentle Puck, come hither. Thou rememberest
That very time I saw, but thou couldst not,
Flying between the cold moon and the earth,
Cupid all armed? A certain aim he took
And marked I where the bolt of Cupid fell.
It fell upon a little western flower –
Before milk-white, now purple with love's wound.
And maidens call it 'Love-in-idleness'.
Fetch me that flower, the herb I showed thee once.
The juice of it on sleeping eyelids laid
Will make or man or woman[2] madly dote
Upon the next live creature that it sees.
Fetch me this herb, and be thou here again
Ere the leviathan[3] can swim a league.

Puck: I'll put a girdle round about the earth
In forty minutes.

Puck quickly runs off

Oberon: Having once this juice
I'll watch Titania when she is asleep,
And drop the liquor of it in her eyes.
The next thing then she waking looks upon,
Be it on lion, bear, or wolf, or bull,
On meddling monkey, or on busy ape,
She shall pursue it with the soul of love.

---

[1] stay away from the places you usually go to   [2] either man or woman   [3] whale

> And ere I take this charm off from her sight,
> As I can take it with another herb,
> I'll make her render up her page to me.
> But who comes here? I am invisible,
> And I will overhear their conference.

Demetrius walks on, followed by Helena. They can't see Oberon

Demetrius: I love thee not, therefore pursue me not.
Where is Lysander and fair Hermia?
The one I'll slay, the other slayeth me.
Thou told'st me they were stolen[1] into this wood.
Hence, get thee gone, and follow me no more.

Helena: You draw me, you hard-hearted adamant[2].

Demetrius: Do I entice you? Do I speak you fair?
Or, rather, do I not in plainest truth
Tell you I do not nor I cannot love you?

Helena: And even for that do I love you the more.
I am your spaniel, and, Demetrius,
The more you beat me, I will fawn[3] on you.

Demetrius: Tempt not too much the hatred of my spirit,
For I am sick when I do look on you.

Helena: And I am sick when I look not on you.

Demetrius: I'll run from thee and hide me in the brakes[4],
And leave thee to the mercy of wild beasts.
Or, if thou follow me, do not believe
But I shall do thee mischief in the wood.

Demetrius strides off, Helena speaks as she chases after him

Helena: Ay, in the temple, in the town, the field,
You do me mischief. Fie, Demetrius!
Your wrongs do set a scandal on my sex.
We cannot fight for love, as men may do.
We should be wooed and were not made to woo.
I'll follow thee and make a heaven of hell,
To die upon the hand I love so well.

---

[1] sneaked [2] magnet [3] worship [4] bushes

A Propeller production by the Watermill Theatre, directed by Edward Hall, photo: Richard Termine

Oberon: Fare thee well, nymph. Ere he do leave this grove,
Thou shalt fly him, and he shall seek thy love.

Puck comes back

Hast thou the flower there? Welcome, wanderer.

Puck: Ay, there it is.

Oberon: I pray thee, give it me.
I know a bank where the wild thyme blows,
Where oxlips and the nodding violet grows,
Quite over-canopied with lush woodbine,
With sweet musk-roses and with eglantine.
There sleeps Titania sometime of the night,
Lulled in these flowers with dances and delight,
And with the juice of this I'll streak her eyes,
And make her full of hateful fantasies.

Oberon leads Puck aside, talking quietly as the Narrators speak

Narrator 2: As you can see Puck is Oberon's most trusted servant. He may be famous for playing silly tricks and frightening the village maids, but for his king, he can fetch a magical flower from far away in just a few minutes.

Narrator 1: And with the juice from this flower, Oberon can cast a spell on his wife, making her fall in love with the first living thing she sees, whatever it is?

Narrator 2: That's his plan. And then he can get the changeling from her.

Narrator 1: I see. And haven't I just heard Oberon say that he would make sure Demetrius ends up chasing Helena rather than her chasing him?

Narrator 2: Yes, Oberon does seem to feel sorry for her.

Oberon returns with Puck and gives him a flower

Oberon: Take thou some of it, and seek through this grove.
A sweet Athenian lady is in love
With a disdainful youth. Anoint his eyes,
But do it when the next thing he espies
May be the lady. Thou shalt know the man
By the Athenian garments he hath on.

Puck: Fear not, my lord, your servant shall do so.

Oberon and Puck leave in different directions

Act 2 Scene 2

Another part of the woods

Titania comes on followed by her fairy attendants. She lays down to sleep on a bed of flowers

Titania: Come now a fairy song. Sing me asleep.

Fairies: *(Singing)* You spotted snakes with double tongue,
Thorny hedge-hogs, be not seen.
Newts, and blind-worms, do no wrong,
Come not near our fairy queen.
Philomel[1], with melody,
Sing in our sweet lullaby;
Lulla, lulla, lullaby, lulla, lulla, lullaby.
Never harm,
Nor spell, nor charm,
Come our lovely lady nigh.
So, good night, with lullaby.

---

[1] the nightingale

The fairies all creep away. Titania is sleeping. Oberon enters and squeezes the flower on Titania's eyelids

Oberon: What thou seest when thou dost wake,
Do it for thy true-love take.
When thou wak'st, it is thy dear.
Wake when some vile thing is near.

Oberon leaves. Lysander and Hermia stagger into this part of the wood, but cannot see the fairies

Lysander: Fair love, you faint with wandering in the wood,
And to speak truth, I have forgot our way.
We'll rest us, Hermia, if you think it good,
And tarry for the comfort of the day.

Hermia: Be it so, Lysander. Find you out a bed,
For I upon this bank will rest my head.

Hermia lays down on the grass and Lysander sits beside her

Lysander: One turf shall serve as pillow for us both;
One heart, one bed, two bosoms, and one troth.[1]

Hermia: Nay, gentle friend, for love and courtesy
Lie further off, in human modesty,
Such separation as may well be said
Becomes a virtuous bachelor and a maid.

Lysander is reluctant to leave Hermia's side but understands her feelings. He finds another piece of grass to lie on

Lysander: Here is my bed. Sleep give thee all his rest.

Hermia and Lysander both fall asleep. Puck comes on

Puck: Through the forest have I gone,
But Athenian found I none.

Puck notices first Lysander and then Hermia

This is he, my master said,
Despised the Athenian maid,
And here the maiden, sleeping sound,
On the dank and dirty ground.

---

[1] promise to be true

The Shorter Shakespeare   *Act 2 Scene 2*

Puck squeezes the flower on Lysander's eyelids
> So awake when I am gone,
> For I must now to Oberon.

Puck runs off. Demetrius and Helena come running on

Helena: Stay, though thou kill me, sweet Demetrius.

Demetrius: I charge thee, hence, and do not haunt me thus.

Demetrius runs off. Helena is too out of breath to follow him

Helena: Happy is Hermia, wheresoe'er she lies,
For she hath blessed and attractive eyes.
How came her eyes so bright? Not with salt tears –
If so, my eyes are oftener washed than hers.
No, no, I am as ugly as a bear,
For beasts that meet me run away for fear.

She notices Lysander sleeping on the ground
> But who is here? Lysander, on the ground?
> Dead, or asleep? I see no blood, no wound.
> Lysander, if you live, good sir, awake.

Helena wakes Lysander

Lysander: And run through fire I will for thy sweet sake.
Where is Demetrius? O, how fit a word
Is that vile name to perish on my sword.

Helena: Do not say so, Lysander, say not so.
What though he love your Hermia? Lord, what though?
Yet Hermia still loves you, then be content.

Lysander: Content with Hermia? No, I do repent
The tedious minutes I with her have spent.
Not Hermia, but Helena I love.
Who will not change a raven for a dove?
The will of man is by his reason swayed,
And reason says you are the worthier maid.

Lysander takes Helena in his arms. She struggles free

Helena: Wherefore was I to this keen mockery born?
When at your hands did I deserve this scorn?
Is't not enough, is't not enough, young man,

Act 2 Scene 2 *The Shorter Shakespeare*

Helena resisting Lysander, RSC production, photo: John Haynes © Royal Shakespeare Company

>   That I did never, no, nor never can,
>   Deserve a sweet look from Demetrius' eye,
>   But you must flout my insufficiency?[1]
>   But fare you well. Perforce I must confess
>   I thought you lord of more true gentleness.

Helena runs off

Lysander: *(to himself)*
>   She sees not Hermia. Hermia, sleep thou there;
>   And never mayst thou come Lysander near.
>   And, all my powers, address your love and might
>   To honour Helen, and to be her knight.

Lysander runs after Helena. Hermia starts to wake up from a nightmare

Hermia: Help me, Lysander, help me! Do thy best
>   To pluck this crawling serpent from my breast.
>   Ay me, for pity. What a dream was here.
>   Lysander, look how I do quake with fear.

Hermia looks around for Lysander

>   Lysander? What, removed? – Lysander, lord?
>   What, out of hearing? Gone? No sound, no word?
>   No? Then I well perceive you are not nigh.
>   Either death or you I'll find immediately.

Hermia runs off

Narrator 2: Now you see the fun Puck can make with his magic.

Narrator 1: It's not fun for Helena and Hermia. They're both confused and frightened by Lysander's strange behaviour.

Narrator 2: Yes, think how odd it looks to Helena – she doesn't know about the magic flower so she thinks Lysander is mocking her by pretending to be in love with her.

Narrator 1: And think about Hermia. When she went to sleep Lysander was madly in love with her and couldn't get close enough. Now he's disappeared.

Narrator 2: And just to add to the confusion here is the group of workmen we saw earlier. They're going to rehearse right next to where the fairy queen is sleeping. Soon you'll really see just how mischievous Puck can be.

---

[1] laugh at me for not being good enough for Demetrius

Act 3 Scene 1

The same part of the wood

Quince, Snug, Bottom, Flute, Snout, and Starveling come on

Bottom: Are we all met?

Quince: Here's a marvellous convenient place for our rehearsal. This green plot shall be our stage.

Bottom: Peter Quince?

Quince: What sayst thou, bully[1] Bottom?

Bottom: There are things in this comedy of Pyramus and Thisbe that will never please. First, Pyramus must draw a sword to kill himself, which the ladies cannot abide. How answer you that?

Starveling: I believe we must leave the killing out, when all is done.

Bottom: Not a whit. I have a device to make all well. Write me a prologue, and let the prologue seem to say we will do no harm with our swords, and that Pyramus is not killed indeed; and, for the more better assurance, tell them that I, Pyramus, am not Pyramus, but Bottom the weaver. This will put them out of fear.

Quince: Well, we will have such a prologue.

Snout: Will not the ladies be afeard of the lion?

Starveling: I fear it, I promise you.

Bottom: Masters, a lion among ladies, is a most dreadful thing, for there is not a more fearful wild fowl than your lion living, and we ought to look to it.

Snout: Therefore, another prologue must tell he is not a lion.

Bottom: Nay, you must name his name, and half his face must be seen and he himself must speak, saying thus, or to the same defect: 'Ladies,' or, 'Fair ladies,' 'I would wish you,' or, 'I would request you,' or, 'I would entreat

---

[1] friend, mate

you, not to fear, not to tremble. If you think I come hither as a lion, it were pity of my life. No, I am no such thing. I am a man as other men are' – and there, indeed, let him name his name, and tell them plainly he is Snug the joiner.

Quince: Well, it shall be so. But there is two hard things: that is, to bring the moonlight into a chamber – for, you know, Pyramus and Thisbe meet by moonlight.

Snug: Doth the moon shine that night we play our play?

Bottom: A calendar, a calendar! Find out moonshine, find out moonshine.

Quince looks in a book. Puck comes on, invisible to the workmen, and watches them, amused

Quince: Yes, it doth shine that night.

Bottom: Why, then may you leave a casement of the great chamber window, where we play, open and the moon may shine in at the casement.

Quince: Ay, or else one must come in with a bush of thorns[1] and a lantern, and say he comes to present the person of Moonshine. Then, there is another thing: we must have a wall in the great chamber, for Pyramus and Thisbe, says the story, did talk through the chink of a wall.

Snug: You can never bring in a wall. What say you, Bottom?

Bottom: Some man or other must present Wall – and let him have some plaster about him, to signify 'wall' – and let him hold his fingers thus, *(Bottom makes a 'V' with his fingers)* and through that cranny shall Pyramus and Thisbe whisper.

Quince: If that may be, then all is well. Come, sit down, every mother's son, and rehearse your parts. Pyramus, you begin, and so every one according to his cue.

---

[1] traditionally, the man in the moon had a bundle of twigs for firewood and also a dog

Puck: *(to the audience)*
What hempen homespuns[1] have we swaggering here
So near the cradle of the Fairy Queen?

Quince: Speak, Pyramus. Thisbe, stand forth.

Bottom: Thisbe, the flowers of odours savours sweet.
So hath thy breath, my dearest Thisbe dear.
But hark, a voice. Stay thou but here a while,
And by and by I will to thee appear.

Bottom leaves the 'stage area' to wait out of sight. Puck follows him

Flute: Must I speak now?

Quince: Ay, for you must understand, he goes but to see a noise that he heard, and is to come again.

Flute: *(speaking in a girl's voice)*
Most radiant Pyramus, most lily-white of hue,
Of colour like the red rose on triumphant briar.
Most brisky juvenal[2], and eke most lovely Jew[3],
As true as truest horse that yet would never tire.
I'll meet thee, Pyramus, at Ninny's tomb.

Quince: 'Ninus' tomb, man! Why, you must not speak that yet. That you answer to Pyramus. You speak all your part at once, cues and all. Pyramus, enter: your cue is past; it is 'never tire.'

Flute: O – As true as truest horse, that yet would never tire.

Bottom returns, but now has the head of a donkey. Puck follows him laughing

Bottom: If I were fair, Thisbe, I were only thine.

Quince: O monstrous! O strange! We are haunted. Pray, masters; fly, masters – help!

The workmen run off screaming at the sight of Bottom. He stands staring in amazement at their actions. Puck, still invisible to Bottom, dances around him, laughing, and then runs off

---

[1] country bumpkins dressed in rough clothes   [2] lively young man   [3] the word is there just for the rhyme

The Shorter Shakespeare *Act 3 Scene 1*

Russ Abbot as Bottom, 2004, Open Air Theatre, Regent's Park, London, photo: Alistair Muir

Bottom: Why do they run away? I see their knavery. This is to make an ass of me, to fright me, if they could. But I will not stir from this place, do what they can. I will walk up and down here, and I will sing, that they shall hear I am not afraid.

Bottom sings loudly in a braying, tuneless voice and his singing wakes up the fairy queen

Titania: What angel wakes me from my flowery bed?

Titania sees Bottom and listens with an expression of love on her face until his song finishes

Titania: I pray thee, gentle mortal, sing again.
Mine ear is much enamoured of thy note.
So is mine eye enthralled to thy shape,
And thy fair virtue's force[1], perforce, doth move me,
On the first view, to say, to swear, I love thee.

Bottom: Methinks, mistress, you should have little reason for that. And yet, to say the truth, reason and love keep little company together nowadays.

Titania: Thou art as wise as thou art beautiful.

Bottom: Not so, neither; but if I had wit enough to get out of this wood, I have enough to serve mine own turn.

Titania: Out of this wood do not desire to go.
Thou shalt remain here, whether thou wilt or no.
I am a spirit of no common rate.
The summer still doth tend upon my state;[2]
And I do love thee. Therefore, go with me.
I'll give thee fairies to attend on thee,
And they shall fetch thee jewels from the deep,
And sing, while thou on pressed flowers dost sleep.
Peaseblossom, Cobweb, Moth, and Mustardseed!

Four fairies suddenly appear

---

[1] all your good qualities   [2] Titania's position as Queen

Peaseblossom: Ready

Cobweb: And I.

Moth: And I.

Mustardseed: And I.

All Four: Where shall we go?

Titania: Be kind and courteous to this gentleman.
Feed him with apricots and dewberries,
With purple grapes, green figs, and mulberries.
The honey-bags steal from the humble-bees,
And pluck the wings from painted butterflies
To fan the moonbeams from his sleeping eyes.
Nod to him, elves, and do him courtesies.

The fairies bow to Bottom, who nods in turn to them

Come, wait upon him; lead him to my bower.

Titania leaves and the fairies lead Bottom to follow her

Act 3 Scene 2

Another part of the Wood

Oberon comes in

Oberon: I wonder if Titania be awaked,
Then, what it was that next came in her eye,
Which she must dote on in extremity.
Here comes my messenger.

Puck comes in

How now, mad spirit?
What night-rule[1] now about this haunted grove?

Puck: My mistress with a monster is in love.
Near to her close and consecrated bower,
While she was in her dull and sleeping hour,
A crew of patches, rude mechanicals[2],
That work for bread upon Athenian stalls[3],
Were met together to rehearse a play

---

[1] night-time fun [2] rough, uncouth workmen in patched clothes [3] workshops

Intended for great Theseus' nuptial day.
The shallowest thick-skin of that barren sort[1],
Who Pyramus presented, in their sport
Forsook his scene and entered in a brake,
When I did him at this advantage take:
An ass's nole I fixed on his head.
Anon his Thisbe must be answered,
And forth my mimic comes. When they him spy
So at his sight away his fellows fly.
I led them on in this distracted fear,
And left sweet Pyramus translated there;
When in that moment, so it came to pass,
Titania waked and straightway loved an ass.

Oberon: This falls out better than I could devise.
But hast thou yet latched the Athenian's eyes
With the love-juice, as I did bid thee do?

Puck: I took him sleeping; that is finished too,
And the Athenian woman by his side,
That, when he waked, of force she must be eyed.

Demetrius and Hermia come on, arguing. They cannot see the fairies

Oberon: Stand close. This is the same Athenian.

Puck: This is the woman, but not this the man.

Oberon and Puck stand back to watch the lovers

Demetrius: O, why rebuke you him that loves you so?

Hermia: If thou hast slain Lysander in his sleep,
Being o'er shoes in blood, plunge in knee deep,
And kill me too.

Demetrius: You spend your passion on a misprised mood.[2]
I am not guilty of Lysander's blood,
Nor is he dead, for aught that I can tell.

Hermia: I pray thee, tell me then that he is well.

---

[1] dull, not very bright [2] you're mistaken to be so angry with me

The Shorter Shakespeare Act 3 Scene 2

Guthrie Theater, photo: Michal Daniel

Demetrius: And if I could, what should I get therefore?

Hermia: A privilege never to see me more.
And from thy hated presence part I so.
See me no more, whether he be dead or no.

Hermia storms off

Demetrius: There is no following her in this fierce vein.
Here, therefore, for a while I will remain.

Demetrius lies down and falls asleep

Oberon: What hast thou done? Thou hast mistaken quite,
And laid the love juice on some true love's sight.
About the wood go swifter than the wind,
And Helena of Athens look thou find.
By some illusion see thou bring her here.
I'll charm his eyes against she do appear.

Puck: I go, I go – look how I go,
Swifter than arrow from the Tartar's[1] bow.

Puck quickly runs off

Oberon: Flower of this purple dye,
Hit with Cupid's archery,
Sink in apple of his eye.

Oberon squeezes another of the magic flowers on to Demetrius' eyelids

When his love he doth espy,
Let her shine as gloriously
As the Venus of the sky.

Puck runs back on

Puck: Captain of our fairy band,
Helena is here at hand,
And the youth, mistook by me.
Shall we their fond pageant[2] see?
Lord, what fools these mortals be!

Oberon: Stand aside. The noise they make
Will cause Demetrius to awake.

---

[1] the Tartars were fierce warriors   [2] foolish show

Puck: *(delighted)* Then will two at once woo one.

Helena walks on wearily with Lysander following

Lysander: How can these things in me seem scorn to you,
Bearing the badge of faith to prove them true?

Helena: These vows are Hermia's. Will you give her o'er?

Lysander: I had no judgment when to her I swore.
Demetrius loves her, and he loves not you.

Demetrius is awakened by their arguing and sees Helena.

Demetrius: O Helen, goddess, nymph, perfect, divine!
To what, my love, shall I compare thine eyne?
Crystal is muddy. O how ripe in show
Thy lips, those kissing cherries, tempting grow.

Helena: O spite! O hell! I see you all are bent
To set against me for your merriment.
If you were civil and knew courtesy,
You would not do me thus much injury.
Can you not hate me, as I know you do,
But you must join in souls to mock me too?
If you were men, as men you are in show,
You would not use a gentle lady so.

Lysander: You are unkind, Demetrius. Be not so.
For you love Hermia – this you know I know –
And here, with all good will, with all my heart,
In Hermia's love I yield you up my part.
And yours of Helena to me bequeath,
Whom I do love, and will do to my death.

Helena: Never did mockers waste more idle breath.

Demetrius: Lysander, keep thy Hermia. I will none.
If e'er I loved her, all that love is gone.
My heart with her but as guestwise sojourned,[1]
And now to Helen it is home returned,
There to remain.

---

[1] stayed as a visitor

Lysander: Helen, it is not so.

Demetrius: Look where thy love comes; yonder is thy dear.

Hermia runs on, relieved to have found Lysander

Hermia: Dark night, that from the eye his function takes,
The ear more quick of apprehension makes[1].
Thou art not by mine eye, Lysander, found,
Mine ear, I thank it, brought me to thy sound.
But why unkindly didst thou leave me so?

Lysander: Why should he stay, whom love doth press to go?

Hermia: What love could press Lysander from my side?

Lysander: Lysander's love, that would not let him bide.
Fair Helena, who more engilds the night
Than all yon fiery oes and eyes of light.[2]
Why seek'st thou me? Could not this make thee know,
The hate I bear thee made me leave thee so?

Hermia: You speak not as you think. It cannot be.

Helena: *(to the audience and then to Hermia)*
Lo, she is one of this confederacy.
Now I perceive they have conjoined all three
To fashion this false sport in spite of me.
Injurious Hermia, most ungrateful maid
Have you conspired? O, is all quite forgot?
All schooldays' friendship, childhood innocence?
We, Hermia, like two artificial gods[3],
Have with our needles created both one flower,
Both on one sampler, sitting on one cushion,
Both warbling of one song, both in one key,
As if our hands, our sides, voices, and minds,
Had been incorporate[4]. So we grew together,
So, with two seeming bodies, but one heart.
And will you rent our ancient love asunder[5],
To join with men in scorning your poor friend?
It is not friendly, 'tis not maidenly.

---

[1] night-time takes sight away but makes hearing more sensitive [2] sparkling star
[3] gods good at creating things [4] part of one body [5] tear our long friendship apart

	Our sex, as well as I, may chide you for it,
	Though I alone do feel the injury.
Hermia:	I am amazed at your passionate words.
	I scorn you not. It seems that you scorn me.
Helena:	Have you not set Lysander, as in scorn,
	To follow me, and praise my eyes and face?
	And made your other love, Demetrius –
	Who even but now did spurn me with his foot –
	To call me goddess, nymph, divine and rare,
	Precious, celestial? Wherefore speaks he this
	To her he hates? And wherefore doth Lysander
	Deny your love, so rich within his soul,
	And tender me, forsooth, affection,
	But by your setting on, by your consent?
Hermia:	I understand not what you mean by this.
Helena:	Ay, do. Persever[1], counterfeit[2] sad looks,
	Make mouths upon me when I turn my back,
	Wink each at other, hold the sweet jest up.
	If you have any pity, grace, or manners,
	You would not make me such an argument.
	But, fare ye well. 'Tis partly mine own fault,
	Which death or absence soon shall remedy.
Lysander:	Stay, gentle Helena, hear my excuse.
	My love, my life, my soul, fair Helena!
Helena:	*(sarcastically)* O excellent.
Lysander:	Helen, I love thee, by my life, I do.
Demetrius:	I say I love thee more than he can do.
Lysander:	If thou say so, withdraw[3], and prove it too.
Demetrius:	Quick, come.

Demetrius begins to walk off and Lysander goes to follow him but is held back by Hermia

Hermia: Lysander, whereto tends all this?

---

[1] persist   [2] fake   [3] move away (so they can fight)

Lysander: Hang off, thou cat, thou burr! Vile thing, let loose,
Or I will shake thee from me like a serpent.

Hermia: Why are you grown so rude? What change is this,
Sweet love?

Lysander: Thy love? Out, out!

Hermia: Do you not jest?

Helena: Yes, sooth, and so do you.

Lysander tries to shake off Hermia

Lysander: Demetrius, I will keep my word with thee.

Demetrius: A weak bond[1] holds you. I'll not trust your word.

Lysander: What, should I hurt her, strike her, kill her dead?
Although I hate her, I'll not harm her so.

Hermia: What? Can you do me greater harm than hate?
Hate me? Wherefore? O me, what news, my love?
Am not I Hermia? Are not you Lysander?
I am as fair now as I was erewhile.
Since night you loved me, yet since night you left me.
Why then, you left me – O, the gods forbid –
In earnest, shall I say?

Lysander: Ay, by my life,
And never did desire to see thee more.
Therefore be out of hope, of question, of doubt,
Be certain, nothing truer – 'tis no jest
That I do hate thee and love Helena.

Hermia lets go of Lysander and turns on Helena

Hermia: O me, you juggler[2], you canker blossom[3],
You thief of love – what, have you come by night
And stolen my love's heart from him?

Helena: Fine, i' faith.
Have you no modesty, no maiden shame?
Fie, fie! you counterfeit, you puppet[4] you.

---

[1] a bond is a contract or a promise but here it is also Hermia's arms   [2] trickster
[3] diseased flower   [4] Helena is accusing Hermia of betraying their friendship; Hermia takes this as an insult to her height

Hermia: Puppet? Why so? Ay, that way goes the game.
Now I perceive that she hath made compare
Between our statures; she hath urged her height,
And with her personage, her tall personage,
Her height, forsooth, she hath prevailed with him.
And are you grown so high in his esteem,
Because I am so dwarfish and so low?
How low am I, thou painted maypole? Speak,
How low am I? I am not yet so low
But that my nails can reach unto thine eyes.

Hermia rushes at Helena, who runs away from her and hides behind the men

Photo: Carol Rosegg. The Shakespeare Theatre, Washington, USA 1999. Erik Sorensen as Demetrius, Tricia Paoluccio as Hermia, Gregory Wooddell as Lysander, Anna Cody as Helena and (in background) Andrew Long as Oberon and Blair Singer as Puck. Director: Joe Calarco.

Helena: I pray you, though you mock me, gentlemen,
Let her not hurt me. You perhaps may think,
Because she is something lower than myself,
That I can match her –

Hermia: Lower? Hark, again.

Helena: Good Hermia, do not be so bitter with me.
I evermore did love you, Hermia,
Did ever keep your counsels, never wronged you –
Save that, in love unto Demetrius,
I told him of your stealth unto this wood.
He followed you; for love I followed him.
But he hath chid me hence, and threatened me
To strike me, spurn me, nay, to kill me too.
And now, so you will let me quiet go,
To Athens will I bear my folly back,
And follow you no further. Let me go.

Hermia: Why, get you gone. Who is't that hinders you?

Helena: A foolish heart, that I leave here behind.

Hermia: What, with Lysander?

Helena: With Demetrius.

Lysander: Be not afraid, she shall not harm thee, Helena.

Helena: She was a vixen when she went to school,
And though she be but little, she is fierce.

Hermia: 'Little' again? Nothing but 'low' and 'little'?
Why will you suffer her to flout me thus?
Let me come to her.

Hermia tries to grab Helena again but is pushed away by Lysander

Lysander: Get you gone, you dwarf

Hermia is shocked into silence by Lysander's words and actions

Lysander: *(to Demetrius)* Now follow, if thou dar'st, to try whose right,
Of thine or mine, is most in Helena.

Demetrius: Follow? Nay, I'll go with thee, cheek by jowl.

Demetrius and Lysander walk purposefully off, neither letting the other get in front. Hermia stares at Helena, who is shaking

Helena: Your hands than mine are quicker for a fray,
My legs are longer though, to run away.

Helena runs off

Hermia: I am amazed, and know not what to say.

Hermia shakes her head and walks off. Oberon and Puck come forward

Oberon: This is thy negligence. Still thou mistak'st,
Or else commit'st thy knaveries wilfully.

Puck: Believe me, king of shadows, I mistook.
Did not you tell me I should know the man
By the Athenian garments he had on?
And so far am I glad it so did sort,
As this their jangling I esteem a sport.

Oberon: Thou seest these lovers seek a place to fight
Hie therefore, Robin, overcast the night,
And lead these testy[1] rivals so astray,
As one come not within another's way.
Till o'er their brows death-counterfeiting sleep
With leaden legs and batty wings doth creep.
Then crush this herb into Lysander's eye,
Whose liquor hath this virtuous property,
To take from thence all error with his might,
And make his eyeballs roll with wonted[2] sight.
When they next wake, all this derision
Shall seem a dream and fruitless vision.
Whiles I in this affair do thee employ,
I'll to my queen and beg her Indian boy.
And then I will her charmed eye release
From monster's view, and all things shall be peace.

---

[1] quarrelling, spoiling for a fight [2] normal

Puck: My fairy lord, this must be done with haste,
For night's swift dragons cut the clouds full fast,
And yonder shines Aurora's harbinger,[1]
At whose approach, ghosts, wandering here and there,
Troop home to churchyards, damned spirits all.

Oberon: But we are spirits of another sort.
I with the morning's love have oft made sport.
But, notwithstanding, haste, make no delay.
We may effect this business yet ere day.

Oberon leaves

Puck: Up and down, up and down,
I will lead them up and down.
I am feared in field and town.
Goblin, lead them up and down.
Here comes one.

Lysander walks on, looking around him. The humans cannot see Puck, but he allows them to hear his disguised voice

Lysander: Where art thou, proud Demetrius? Speak thou now.

Puck: *(pretending to be Demetrius)* Here, villain, drawn and ready. Where art thou?

Lysander: I will be with thee straight.

Puck: *(pretending to be Demetrius)* Follow me, then,
To plainer ground.

Lysander walks off following the voice he has heard. Demetrius comes on from a different direction

Demetrius: Lysander, speak again.
Thou runaway, thou coward, art thou fled?

Puck: *(pretending to be Lysander)*
Thou coward, art thou bragging to the stars,
And wilt not come? Come, recreant,[2] come, thou child.

Demetrius runs off believing he is chasing Lysander. Lysander re-enters, now looking tired

---

[1] the morning star which shows that dawn (Aurora) is coming   [2] coward

Lysander: The villain is much lighter heeled than I.
I followed fast, but faster he did fly.
That fallen am I in dark uneven way,
And here will rest me.

Lysander lies down

Come, thou gentle day.
For if but once thou show me thy grey light,
I'll find Demetrius and revenge this spite.

Lysander falls asleep. Puck comes back leading Demetrius, who does not see Lysander

Puck: *(pretending to be Lysander)*
Ho, ho, ho, coward, why com'st thou not?

Demetrius: Thou runn'st before me, shifting every place,
And dar'st not stand, nor look me in the face.
If ever I thy face by daylight see –
Now, go thy way. Faintness constraineth me
To measure out my length on this cold bed.
By day's approach look to be visited.

Demetrius lies down to sleep. Helena comes on, but does not notice Lysander or Demetrius

Helena: O weary night, O long and tedious night,
Abate[1] thy hours; shine comforts from the east
That I may back to Athens by daylight,
From these that my poor company detest.
And sleep, that sometimes shuts up sorrow's eye,
Steal me a while from mine own company.

Helena lays down and falls asleep

Puck: Yet but three? Come one more,
Two of both kinds make up four.
Here she comes, curst and sad.
Cupid is a knavish lad,
Thus to make poor females mad.

Hermia trudges on, not noticing the other three lovers

---

[1] shorten

Act 3 Scene 2					The Shorter Shakespeare

Guthrie Theater, photo: Michal Daniel

Hermia: Never so weary, never so in woe,
Bedabbled with the dew and torn with briars,
I can no further crawl, no further go.
My legs can keep no pace with my desires.
Here will I rest me till the break of day.
Heavens shield Lysander, if they mean a fray.

Hermia sinks to the ground and falls asleep

Puck: On the ground,
Sleep sound.
I'll apply, to your eye,
Gentle lover, remedy

Puck squeezes the juice of another magic flower on to Lysander's eyelids

And the country proverb known,
That every man should take his own,
In your waking shall be shown.
Jack shall have Jill,
Nought shall go ill.
The man shall have his mare again,
And all shall be well.

Puck leaves the lovers sleeping

Narrator 1: So it seems Puck has finally sorted out the lovers.

Narrator 2: When they wake, they'll believe all their arguments were just a rather strange bad dream.

Narrator 1: But what about Titania and Bottom?

Narrator 2: While Titania was under the influence of the juice of the magic flower, she loved Bottom even though he looked like a monster and she put a crown of flowers over his donkey ears. Of course Bottom, himself, still didn't realise that he'd been changed.

Narrator 1: Poor Titania. And the changeling?

Narrator 2: Oh, she was so obsessed with her new love that she easily gave up the Indian boy when Oberon asked her for him again. Now she is tired and ready to sleep.

Act 4 Scene 1

The same part of the wood

The lovers are lying on the ground, fast asleep. Titania comes on with Bottom, who still has his donkey's head. They are followed by fairy attendants

Titania: Come, sit thee down upon this flowery bed,
And stick musk-roses in thy sleek smooth head,

Titania and Bottom sit down together

Bottom: Where's Peaseblossom?

Peaseblossom: Ready.

Bottom: Scratch my head, Peaseblossom. Where's Monsieur Cobweb?

Cobweb: Ready.

Bottom: Monsieur Cobweb, good monsieur, kill me a redhipped humble-bee on the top of a thistle, and, good monsieur, bring me the honey-bag. Where's Monsieur Mustardseed?

Mustardseed: Ready.

Bottom: Good monsieur, help Peaseblossom to scratch. I must to the barber's, monsieur, for methinks I am marvellous hairy about the face.

Titania: What, wilt thou hear some music, my sweet love?
Or say, sweet love, what thou desir'st to eat.

Bottom: Truly, I could munch your good dry oats. Methinks I have a great desire to good hay, sweet hay. But, I pray you, let none of your people stir me. I have an exposition of sleep come upon me.

The Shorter Shakespeare .... Act 4 Scene 1

Titania and Bottom (Amy Rockson & Chris Donnelly), Shakespeare at the Tobacco Factory, photo by Toby Farrow

Titania: Sleep thou, and I will wind thee in my arms.
　　　　　Fairies, be gone, and be all ways away.
The fairy attendants leave Titania and Bottom alone. Titania embraces Bottom
　　　　　O how I love thee, how I dote on thee.
Titania and Bottom fall asleep in each other's arms. Oberon and Puck both come on, but from different directions

Oberon: Welcome, good Robin. See'st thou this sweet sight?
　　　　　Her dotage now I do begin to pity.
　　　　　And now I have the boy, I will undo
　　　　　This hateful imperfection of her eyes.
　　　　　And, gentle Puck, take this transformed scalp
　　　　　From off the head of this Athenian swain[1],
　　　　　That he, awaking when the other do,
　　　　　May all to Athens back again repair,
　　　　　And think no more of this night's accidents
　　　　　But as the fierce vexation of a dream.
　　　　　But first I will release the fairy queen.
Oberon squeezes the juice of the second magic flower on to Titania's eyelids.
　　　　　Be as thou wast wont[2] to be,
　　　　　See as thou wast wont to see.
　　　　　Now, my Titania, wake you, my sweet queen.
Titania awakes, unaware of Bottom beside her

Titania: My Oberon, what visions have I seen!
　　　　　Methought I was enamoured of an ass.

Oberon: There lies your love.
Titania now sees Bottom, with his donkey's head, lying beside her

Titania: How came these things to pass?
　　　　　O, how mine eyes do loathe his visage now.

Oberon: Silence a while. Robin, take off this head.
Puck removes the donkey head from Bottom.

Puck: When thou wak'st, with thine own fool's eyes peep.

---

[1] young man　[2] used

Oberon: Sound music.

Music plays

> Come, my queen, take hands with me,
> And rock the ground whereon these sleepers be.

Oberon and Titania dance

> Now thou and I are new in amity[1],
> And will tomorrow midnight solemnly
> Dance in Duke Theseus' house triumphantly,
> And bless it to all fair prosperity.
> There shall the pairs of faithful lovers be
> Wedded, with Theseus, all in jollity.

Puck: Fairy king, attend, and mark.
> I do hear the morning lark.

Oberon: Then, my queen, in silence sad,
> Trip we after the night's shade.
> We the globe can compass[2] soon,
> Swifter than the wandering moon.

Titania: Come, my lord, and in our flight
> Tell me how it came this night
> That I sleeping here was found
> With these mortals on the ground.

Oberon leads Titania away. Puck follows them

Narrator 2: With the break of day, the fairies are all flying off to follow the moon. They won't return until night falls again. Meanwhile, Theseus and Hippolyta have got up early in order to give thanks to their gods for the summer and for their wedding. They are now on their way to hunt with their hounds in the woods. Hermia's father, Egeus, is with them as are many other nobles and attendants.

Narrator 1: And the young lovers are asleep in the woods. The hunting party is bound to find them!

Theseus, Hippolyta, Egeus and attendants come in dressed for hunting

---

[1] friendship [2] travel round

Egeus: My lord, this is my daughter here asleep,
And this, Lysander, this Demetrius is.
This Helena, old Nedar's Helena.
I wonder of their being here together.

Theseus: No doubt they rose up early to observe
The rite of May,[1] and, hearing our intent,
Came here in grace of our solemnity.[2]
But speak, Egeus, is not this the day
That Hermia should give answer of her choice?

Egeus: It is, my lord.

Theseus: Go, bid the huntsmen wake them with their horns.

The huntsmen blow their horns and the lovers wake up suddenly

Good morrow, friends. Saint Valentine[3] is past.
Begin these wood-birds but to couple now?

Lysander: Pardon, my lord.

Lysander and the others kneel in front of the Duke

Theseus: I pray you all, stand up.
(to Demetrius and Lysander)
I know you two are rival enemies.
How comes this gentle concord in the world,
That hatred is so far from jealousy,
To sleep by hate, and fear no enmity?

Lysander: My lord, I shall reply amazedly,
Half sleep, half waking, but as yet, I swear,
I cannot truly say how I came here.
But, as I think – for truly would I speak,
And now I do bethink me, so it is –
I came with Hermia hither. Our intent
Was to be gone from Athens, where we might,
Without the peril of the Athenian law –

Egeus: Enough, enough, my lord, you have enough.
I beg the law, the law, upon his head.

---

[1] May day traditions   [2] in honour of our wedding celebrations
[3] on St Valentine's day, birds were supposed to choose their mates

They would have stolen away. They would, Demetrius,
Thereby to have defeated you and me;
You of your wife, and me of my consent,
Of my consent that she should be your wife.

Demetrius: My lord, fair Helen told me of their stealth,
Of this their purpose hither, to this wood,
And I in fury hither followed them,
Fair Helena in fancy following me.
But, my good lord, I wot not by what power,
My love to Hermia melted as the snow.
The object and the pleasure of mine eye,
Is only Helena. To her, my lord,
Was I betrothed ere I saw Hermia.
But, like in sickness, did I loathe this food,
But, as in health, come to my natural taste,
Now do I wish it, love it, long for it,
And will for evermore be true to it.

Theseus: Fair lovers, you are fortunately met.
Of this discourse we more will hear anon.
Egeus, I will overbear your will,
For in the temple, by and by, with us,
These couples shall eternally be knit.
Away with us, to Athens, three and three,
We'll hold a feast in great solemnity.
Come, Hippolyta.

Theseus, Hippolyta, Egeus and the attendants leave

Demetrius: Are you sure that we are awake? It seems
The duke was here, and bid us follow him?

Hermia: Yea, and my father.

Helena: And Hippolyta.

Lysander: And he did bid us follow to the temple.

Demetrius: Why then, we are awake. Let's follow him.
And by the way let us recount our dreams.

The lovers follow Theseus. Bottom now wakes up thinking he is still at the rehearsal

Bottom: When my cue comes, call me, and I will answer. My next is, 'Most fair Pyramus.' Heigh-ho. Peter Quince? Flute, the bellows-mender? Snout, the tinker? Starveling? God's my life! Stolen hence, and left me asleep? I have had a most rare vision. I have had a dream, past the wit of man to say what dream it was. Man is but an ass, if he go about to expound this dream. Methought I was – and methought I had – I will get Peter Quince to write a ballad of this dream. It shall be called Bottom's Dream, because it hath no bottom.

Bottom leaves to walk back to Athens

Act 4 Scene 2

Peter Quince's House in Athens

Quince, Flute, Snout and Starveling are sitting quietly together

Quince: Have you sent to Bottom's house? Is he come home yet?

Starveling: He cannot be heard of.

Flute: If he come not, then the play goes not forward, doth it?

Quince: It is not possible. You have not a man in all Athens able to discharge Pyramus but he.

Flute: No, he hath simply the best wit of any handicraft man in Athens.

Quince: Yea, and the best person too.

Snug comes in

Snug: Masters, the duke is coming from the temple, and there is two or three lords and ladies more married. If our sport[1] had gone forward, we had all been made men.[2]

Flute: O sweet bully Bottom! Thus hath he lost sixpence a day during his life. An the duke had not given him sixpence a day for playing Pyramus, I'll be hanged. He would have deserved it.

---

[1] activity [2] our fortunes would have been made

Snug, Quince, Flute, Snout (David Plimmer, Jonathan Nibbs, Byron Mondahl, Felix Hayes), Shakespeare at the Tobacco Factory, photo: Toby Farrow

Bottom comes in

Bottom: Where are these lads? Where are these hearts?

Quince: Bottom! O most courageous day! O most happy hour!

Bottom: Masters, I am to discourse wonders but ask me not what.

Quince: Let us hear, sweet Bottom.

Bottom: Not a word of me. All that I will tell you is that the Duke hath dined. Get your apparel together. Meet presently at the palace, every man look o'er his part. For the short and the long is, our play is preferred.[1] And, most dear actors, eat no onions nor garlic, for we are to utter sweet breath, and I do not doubt but to hear them say it is a sweet comedy. No more words. Away, go, away!

The workmen all rush off

---

[1] chosen

Act 5 Scene 1

The Royal palace in Athens

Narrator 1: Well, everything has worked out for Bottom.

Narrator 2: Yes and we will soon see how he and his friends do when they perform their play at the palace, where there has just been a triple wedding.

Theseus, Hippolyta, Egeus and attendants come in

Hippolyta: 'Tis strange, my Theseus, that these lovers speak of.

Theseus: More strange than true. I never may believe
These antique fables, nor these fairy toys.
Lovers and madmen have such seething brains,
Such shaping fantasies, that apprehend
More than cool reason ever comprehends.
The lunatic, the lover, and the poet,
Are of imagination all compact[1].

Hippolyta: But all their minds transfigured so together?

Hermia, Lysander, Helena and Demetrius come in

Theseus: Here come the lovers, full of joy and mirth.

Greetings and congratulations are exchanged.

Theseus: Come now, what masques,[2] what dances shall we have
To wear away this long age of three hours
Between our after-supper and bed-time?
(to Egeus) Say, what abridgment[3] have you for this evening?
What masque? What music? How shall we beguile[4]
The lazy time, if not with some delight?

Egeus bows and presents a menu of possible entertainments to Theseus who passes the list to Lysander

Egeus: Make choice of which your highness will see first.

Lysander glances down the list and then reads aloud

---

[1] all think the same way   [2] short plays with music and dance
[3] entertainment, something to shorten the time   [4] while away

Lysander: A tedious brief scene of young Pyramus
And his love Thisbe; very tragical mirth.

Theseus: 'Merry' and 'tragical'? 'Tedious' and 'brief'?
That is, hot ice and wonderous strange snow.
(to Egeus) What are they that do play it?

Egeus: Hard-handed men, that work in Athens here.

Theseus: And we will hear it.

Egeus: No, my noble lord,
It is not for you. I have heard it over,
And it is nothing.

Theseus: I will hear that play;
For never anything can be amiss,
When simpleness and duty tender it.
Go, bring them in, and take your places, ladies.

Egeus goes to fetch the workmen and soon returns

Egeus: So please your Grace, the Prologue is addressed[1].

Theseus: Let him approach.

Trumpets are played then Quince comes on as the Prologue

Quince: *(as Prologue)*
If we offend, it is with our good will.
That you should think, we come not to offend,
But with good will. To show our simple skill,
That is the true beginning of our end.
The actors are at hand, and, by their show,
You shall know all that you are like to know.

Hippolyta: He hath played on his prologue like a child on
a recorder – a sound, but not in government[2].

Theseus: His speech was like a tangled chain. Who is next?

Bottom, Flute, Snout, Starveling and Snug come on in their costumes and mime their story as Quince tells it in the prologue

---

[1] ready   [2] control

Act 5 Scene 1 *The Shorter Shakespeare*

Quince: *(as Prologue)*
Gentles, perchance you wonder at this show?
But wonder on, till truth make all things plain.
This man is Pyramus, if you would know;
This beauteous lady Thisbe is, certain.
This man, with lime and rough-cast, doth present
Wall, that vile Wall which did these lovers sunder,
And through Wall's chink, poor souls, they are content
To whisper, at the which let no man wonder.
This man, with lantern, dog, and bush of thorn,
Presenteth Moonshine; for, if you will know,
By moonshine did these lovers think no scorn
To meet at Ninus' tomb, there, there to woo.
This grisly beast, which Lion hight by name,
The trusty Thisbe, coming first by night,

Quince and Snout, Royal Exchange Theatre, Manchester, photo: Steven Vaughan

>   Did scare away, or rather did affright.
>   And, as she fled, her mantle[1] she did fall,
>   Which Lion vile with bloody mouth did stain.
>   Anon comes Pyramus, sweet youth and tall,
>   And finds his trusty Thisbe's mantle slain.
>   Whereat, with blade, with bloody, blameful blade,
>   He bravely broached his boiling bloody breast.
>   And Thisbe, tarrying in mulberry shade,
>   His dagger drew and died. For all the rest,
>   Let Lion, Moonshine, Wall, and lovers twain,
>   At large discourse, while here they do remain.

Bottom, Flute, Starveling and Snug hurry off leaving Snout as the Wall

Theseus: I wonder, if the lion be to speak?

Demetrius: No wonder, my lord – one lion may, when many asses do.

Snout: *(as Wall)*
> In this same interlude it doth befall
> That I, one Snout by name, present a wall,
> And such a wall, as I would have you think,
> That had in it a crannied hole or chink,

Snout holds up his fingers to show the chink

> Through which the lovers, Pyramus and Thisbe,
> Did whisper often very secretly.
> This loam, this rough-cast, and this stone doth show
> That I am that same wall; the truth is so.

Demetrius: It is the wittiest partition that ever I heard, my lord.

Bottom comes forward as Pyramus

Theseus: Pyramus draws near the wall. Silence.

Bottom: *(as Pyramus)*
> O grim-looked night, O night with hue so black,
> O night, which ever art when day is not!
> O night, O night, alack, alack, alack!
> I fear my Thisbe's promise is forgot.

---

[1] shawl

And thou, O wall, O sweet, O lovely wall!
That standest between her father's ground and mine,
Thou wall, O wall, O sweet, and lovely wall!
Show me thy chink to blink through with mine eyne.

Snout holds up his fingers to form the chink

Thanks, courteous wall. Jove shield thee well for this.
But what see I? No Thisbe do I see.
O wicked wall, through whom I see no bliss.
Cursed be thy stones for thus deceiving me!

Theseus: The wall, methinks, being sensible[1], should curse again.

Bottom: No, in truth, sir, he should not. 'Deceiving me,' is Thisbe's cue. She is to enter now, and I am to spy her through the wall. You shall see. Yonder she comes.

Flute comes forward as Thisbe

Flute: *(as Thisbe)*
O wall, full often hast thou heard my moans,
For parting my fair Pyramus and me.
My cherry lips have often kissed thy stones,
Thy stones with lime and hair knit up in thee.

Bottom: *(as Pyramus)*
I see a voice: now will I to the chink,
To spy an I can hear my Thisbe's face.

Flute: *(as Thisbe)*
My love – thou art my love, I think?

Bottom: *(as Pyramus)*
Think what thou wilt, I am thy lover's grace.
O, kiss me through the hole of this vile wall.

Flute: *(as Thisbe)*
I kiss the wall's hole, not your lips at all.

Bottom: *(as Pyramus)*
Wilt thou at Ninny's tomb meet me straightway?

---

[1] having feelings or senses

The Shorter Shakespeare Act 5 Scene 1

Pyramus and Thisbe (Byron Mondahl & Chris Donnelly), Shakespeare at the Tobacco Factory, photo by Toby Farrow

61

Flute: *(as Thisbe)*
'Tide life, 'tide death,[1] I come without delay.

Bottom and Flute leave in different directions

Snout: *(as Wall)*
Thus have I, Wall, my part discharged so,
And, being done, thus Wall away doth go.

Snout leaves

Hippolyta: *(laughing)* This is the silliest stuff that ever I heard.

Snug comes forward as the Lion, followed by Starveling who carries a bush and a lantern and leads a dog. He is Moonshine

Snug: *(as Lion)*
You, ladies, you, whose gentle hearts do fear
The smallest monstrous mouse that creeps on floor,
May now perchance both quake and tremble here,
When lion rough in wildest rage doth roar.
Then know that I, Snug the joiner, am.

Snug lifts his mask to show his real face

Theseus: A very gentle beast, and of a good conscience. Let us listen to the Moon.

Starveling: *(as Moonshine)*
This lantern doth the horned moon present.

Demetrius: He should have worn the horns on his head.

Starveling: *(as Moonshine)*
This lantern doth the horned moon present.
Myself the man i' th' moon do seem to be.

Theseus: This is the greatest error of all the rest. The man should be put into the lantern. How is it else the man i' th' moon?

Demetrius: He dares not come there for the candle.

Hippolyta: I am aweary of this moon: would he would change.

---

[1] come life or death

Starveling: *(as Moonshine)*
All that I have to say, is, to tell you that the lantern is the moon, I, the man in the moon, this thorn-bush, my thorn-bush, and this dog, my dog.

Demetrius: Why, all these should be in the lantern, for all these are in the moon. But, silence, here comes Thisbe.

Flute, as Thisbe, comes back in

Flute: *(as Thisbe)*
This is old Ninny's tomb. Where is my love?

Snug, as Lion, roars. Flute, as Thisbe, drops her shawl and runs off in fright. Snug, as Lion, bites and shakes the shawl

Demetrius: Well roared, Lion.

Theseus: Well run, Thisbe.

Hippolyta: Well shone, Moon. Truly, the moon shines with a good grace.

Theseus: Well moused, Lion.

Demetrius: And then came Pyramus.

Bottom, as Pyramus, comes forward. Snug, as Lion, runs off, leaving the shawl

Lysander: And so the lion vanished.

Bottom: *(as Pyramus)*
Sweet moon, I thank thee for thy sunny beams.
I thank thee, moon, for thy glittering gleams.

He notices the shawl and picks it up

But stay, O spite!
But mark, poor knight,
What dreadful dole[1] is here?
Eyes, do you see?
How can it be?
O dainty duck, O dear!
O, wherefore, Nature, didst thou lions frame?
Since lion vile hath here deflowered my dear?
Which is – no, no – which was the fairest dame

---

[1] sorrow, distress

> That lived, that loved, that liked, that looked with cheer.
> Come tears, confound.
> Out, sword, and wound
> The pap of Pyramus.
> Ay, that left pap,
> Where heart doth hop.
> Thus die I, thus, thus, thus.

He stabs himself

> Now am I dead,
> Now am I fled.
> My soul is in the sky.
> Tongue, lose thy light!
> Moon, take thy flight!

Starveling (as Moonshine) walks off

> Now die, die, die, die, die.

'Pyramus' dies

Theseus: With the help of a surgeon, he might yet recover, and prove an ass.

Hippolyta: How chance Moonshine is gone before Thisbe comes back and finds her lover?

Theseus: She will find him by starlight. Here she comes, and her passion ends the play.

Flute (as Thisbe) comes back

Hippolyta: Methinks she should not use a long one for such a Pyramus. I hope she will be brief.

Flute: *(as Thisbe)*
> Asleep, my love?
> What, dead, my dove?
> O Pyramus, arise!
> Speak, speak! Quite dumb?
> Dead, dead! A tomb
> Must cover thy sweet eyes.
> These lily lips,
> This cherry nose,

> These yellow cowslip cheeks,
> Are gone, are gone.
> Lovers, make moan
> His eyes were green as leeks.
> Tongue, not a word.
> Come, trusty sword.
> Come, blade, my breast imbrue.

'Thisbe' stabs herself

> And farewell, friends;
> Thus Thisbe ends.
> Adieu, adieu, adieu.

'She' dies

Theseus: Moonshine and Lion are left to bury the dead.

Demetrius: Ay, and Wall too.

Bottom jumps up from his 'death'

Bottom: Will it please you to see the epilogue, or to hear a bergomask[1] dance between two of our company?

Theseus: No epilogue, I pray you, for your play needs no excuse. But come, your bergomask.

Bottom and Flute dance. All the workmen come back to take their bow and then leave

Theseus: The iron tongue of midnight hath told twelve. Lovers, to bed; 'tis almost fairy time.

The lovers and their attendants all leave

Narrator 1: I thought he said he didn't believe in fairies?

Narrator 2: He did, but he's right anyway. It is fairy time. The fairies have come to bless the palace. And to say goodbye.

---

[1] country dance

Act 5 Scene 2

Puck comes in

Puck: Now the hungry lion roars,
And the wolf behowls the moon;
Whilst the heavy ploughman snores,
All with weary task fordone[1].
Now the wasted brands[2] do glow,
Whilst the screech-owl, screeching loud,
Puts the wretch that lies in woe
In remembrance of a shroud.
Now it is the time of night
That the graves, all gaping wide,
Every one lets forth his sprite,
In the church-way paths to glide.
And we fairies, that do run
By the triple Hecate's[3] team,
From the presence of the sun,
Following darkness like a dream,
Now are frolic[4]; not a mouse
Shall disturb this hallowed house.
I am sent with broom before,
To sweep the dust behind the door.

Oberon, Titania and all their fairy attendants come in

Oberon: Through the house give glimmering light
By the dead and drowsy fire.
Every elf and fairy sprite
Hop as light as bird from briar.

Titania: Hand in hand, with fairy grace,
Will we sing, and bless this place.

All the fairies sing and dance

Oberon: Now, until the break of day,
Through this house each fairy stray.
To the best bride-bed will we,
Which by us shall blessed be.

---

[1] worn out   [2] burnt-out logs   [3] Goddess of the moon   [4] playful

The Shorter Shakespeare   *Act 5 Scene 2*

Puck, Royal Exchange Theatre, Manchester, photo: Steven Vaughan

Act 5 Scene 2   *The Shorter Shakespeare*

And the issue[1] there create
Ever shall be fortunate.
So shall all the couples three
Ever true in loving be.
With this field-dew consecrate,[2]
Every fairy take his gait,[3]
And each several chamber bless,
Through this palace, with sweet peace;
And the owner of it blest.
Ever shall in safety rest,
Trip away, make no stay,
Meet me all by break of day.

Oberon and Titania leave arm in arm, followed by all the fairies except Puck

Puck: *(to the audience)* If we shadows have offended,
Think but this, and all is mended,
That you have but slumbered here
While these visions did appear.
And this weak and idle theme,
No more yielding but a dream,
Gentles, do not reprehend,
If you pardon, we will mend.
Else the Puck a liar call.
So, good-night unto you all.
Give me your hands, if we be friends,
And Robin shall restore amends.

---

[1] children   [2] Oberon is telling the fairies to sprinkle special holy or magic water to bless the couples   [3] go his way